FASHIONS OF A DECADE
THE
1970s

FASHIONS OF A DECADE
THE 1970s

Jacqueline Herald

Series Editors: Valerie Cumming and
Elane Feldman
Original Illustrations by Robert Price

Facts On File
New York • Oxford

Contents

Introduction   5

1 Rough and Ready   28
2 Nostalgia   32
3 Black Is Beautiful   36
4 Glamour   40
5 Dressed to Clash   44
6 Trash Culture   48
7 Disco Kings and Queens   52
8 The Rebirth of Style   56

Glossary   60
Reading List   61
Acknowledgments   61
Time Chart   62
Index   64

THE 1970s (FASHIONS OF A DECADE SERIES)

Copyright © 1992 by Jacqueline Herald

Facts On File, Inc.
460 Park Avenue South
New York NY 10016

Facts On File books are available at special discounts when purchased in bulk quantities for businesses, associations, institutions or sales promotions. Please call our Special Sales Department in New York at 212/683-2244 (dial 800/322-8755 except in NY, AK or HI).

Text design by Lisa Morris
Jacket design by Lisa Morris
Composition by Latimer Trend & Company Ltd, Plymouth
Manufactured by World Print Ltd
Printed in Hong Kong

10 9 8 7 6 5 4 3 2 1

This book is printed on acid-free paper.

Library of Congress Cataloging-in-Publication Data
Herald, Jacqueline.
  Fashions of a decade.   The 1970s/Jacqueline Herald.
  P.   cm.
  Includes bibliographical references and index.
    Summary: Looks at how the fashions of the 1970s reflected the social, historical and cultural events of that decade.
    ISBN 0–8160–2470–7
    1. Costume—History—20th century—Juvenile literature.
    2. Civilization, Modern—20th century—Juvenile literature.
  [1. Costume—History—20th century.   2. Civilization, Modern—20th century.]   I. Title.
  GT596.H48   1992
  391'.009'047—dc20
                                                              91–44209

THE 70S

It was writer Tom Wolfe who dubbed the seventies the "Me Decade." The problem was, there were lots of "Me"s fighting for a piece of the action. Politically extremist and fundamentalist groups committed acts of terrorism. In terms of dress, fashion magazines declared "anything goes": there were no rules anymore.

Nostalgia and an interest in traditional cultures of the developing world were elements that ran through the decade, from radical chic to punk. Retro styles were promoted by films like *The Great Gatsby* (1974) in which Mia Farrow and Robert Redford wore twenties-style clothes, and the American TV series *Happy Days*, based on the popular film *American Graffiti*, which centered on fifties' teenagers.

The "Me Decade"

As much as fashion tried, elements of past styles were no escape from the real social, political and environmental upheavals of the present. The energy crisis, increasing unemployment and world recession; the civil rights, gay liberation, and women's movements; growing concern over the future of the environment, focusing on ecology and anti-nuclear strategies; demands for political recognition and independence; terrorism, bombing and hijacking; the arrival of the computer microchip – these elements were all reflected in the way people dressed.

The world seemed smaller. Concorde, the first supersonic airplane, took to the skies. Charter lines offering cheap transatlantic travel sprang up, and the American fast-food chains McDonald's and Colonel Sanders' Kentucky Fried Chicken spread across Europe.

Grease, one of several fifties nostalgia films. John Travolta's greased quiff of hair is authentic enough, though the large shirt collar and cut of his draped jacket and stovepipe pants are unmistakably seventies.

Watergate and the Fall of President Nixon

On June 17, 1972, five men were arrested after they attempted to remove bugging devices from the headquarters of the Democratic National Committee in the Watergate building in Washington, DC. The incident was later traced to the offices of U.S. President Richard Nixon and led to a scandal that raged for many years. In May 1974 impeachment hearings against Nixon were opened; the live broadcasts of the Senate Watergate hearings surpassed the soap operas and baseball games in popularity, as millions of Americans tuned in their television sets. In August Nixon resigned, the first U.S. president to do so before the end of his elected term. Nixon's vice president, Gerald Ford, took over at the White House, and granted him a complete pardon for any federal crimes. However, many of Nixon's top aides were sent to prison.

President Richard Nixon's distinct profile kept the cartoonists happy during extensive media coverage of the Watergate scandal.

Workers in protective clothing set off for the zone contaminated by deadly dioxin, following the disastrous chemical explosion at a Seveso, Italy, fertilizer factory.

Environmental Concerns

In 1970, BBC television's *Doomwatch* series attracted a huge audience, covering environmental problems like the smog over New York and Tokyo. The international pollution debate opened up: concern was voiced over lead poisoning from vehicles' exhaust fumes and the threat to the ozone layer. In Seveso, Italy, in 1976 a cloud of dioxin was accidentally leaked from a fertilizer factory; the disaster left people wondering about its long-term effects on local inhabitants' health.

An oil boom in the North Sea was initially greeted with relief, but a huge slick of oil in 1977 increased worries about the world's diminishing natural resources and fueled the political fervor of environmental lobbyists.

In 1970, Americans celebrated the first Earth Day and many joined increasingly active environmental groups. However, the problems they were working against seemed to increase in number. Acid rain began to kill trees and pollute lakes in the U.S. and Canada. Many urban areas, especially Los Angeles, suffered from extremely poor air quality, and water pollution closed beaches on the Great Lakes.

You Are What You Wear

The idea of dress as a system of signs, indicating the life-style and aspirations of the wearer, was taken very seriously in the 1970s. The discipline is known as semiotics. Writings by French semiologist Roland Barthes became required reading in many art colleges that prioritized theory over practice. Italian academic and novelist Umberto Eco wrote wittily about the relationship between the internal experience and external appearance of wearing blue jeans in an essay of 1976, *Lumbar Thought*.

American psychologists discussed the social and political implications of power dressing. Topical magazines of the period discussed the language of status symbols, designers and clothes. Peter York's caustic columns in the British magazine *Harpers and Queen* defined immediately identifiable social "types" like the Sloane Rangers of London, who are somewhat similar to American preppies.

The Vietnam War

The decade opened with a surge of demonstrations against the Vietnam War, in which America had been actively involved since 1964. In May 1970, U.S. forces invaded neutral Cambodia. That month, tension ran high at Ohio's Kent State University when National Guard troops fired on protesting students: four students were shot dead. Following America's devastating bombing campaign against the Vietcong (Communist) forces and North Vietnamese civilians in 1972, a cease-fire between the United States and North Vietnam was signed in early 1973. American civilians and troops were withdrawn, and prisoners of war returned home to a tumultuous welcome. In January of 1973 the highly controversial military draft ended in the United States. Nevertheless, war was not over. In April 1975 the North Vietnamese attack on the South led speedily to the fall of Saigon, when U.S. civilians, and as many Vietnamese as the U.S. helicopters could carry, were airlifted out, while Communist forces completed their takeover of the country. The film *M*A*S*H,* a black comedy set in Korea but obviously referring to Vietnam, satirized and condemned war and the society that instigated it. In 1977 U.S. President Jimmy Carter pardoned most of an estimated 10,000 draft evaders, many of whom had fled to Canada.

Designer hippies from Kensington at the Royal Ascot horse race meeting, 1970 (left).

Sleek and elegant couple wearing fashions by Christian Dior: the conservative face of respectability (right).

The Women's Movement

By the late sixties, "minority" groups – blacks, gays and women – were becoming more visible and audible in the political arena. The publication of feminist texts gathered momentum during the seventies. They often discussed the position of women in society, beginning with the roles of mother, wife and lover. Germaine Greer's *The Female Eunuch*, published in 1971, challenged traditional perceptions of femininity.

Magazines of the period did not just treat women as fashion consumers but took into account new values and life-styles, including careers. The Japanese publication *An An* was launched in March 1970: it covered Western fashion as well as features on food, travel and American ideals of women's independence. The British and U.S. editions of *Cosmopolitan* offered frank advice on sex, how to take the initiative in meeting men, make-up and the body.

Radical feminists, however, were reluctant to discuss fashion. They were readily stereotyped. "Conference and demonstration dress" included T-shirts with slogans, baggy jeans, practical carry-all bags, and buttons in place of jewelry. Hair was worn long or short; either way, it required (and got) minimal maintenance. Shoes were flat and square-toed. Radical women did not shave their underarms or legs, and they wore no bras. You didn't need to follow high fashion to make an impression.

Even so, fashion and fashion photography went on. Feminist magazines like the British *Spare Rib* began to ask who the photographs were for. Men dominated the advertising and photography professions; yet images of women in fashionable dress or promoting a product were mainly looked at by other women. Shopping was mostly done by women (for themselves, their men and their children).

This was a high fashion idea from Louis Feraud's summer 1971 collection.

Both Laura Ashley's Victorian-style country look and Ralph Lauren's Prairie collection had ruffles around the hem and were often worn with a kerchief around the head or neck and laced mid-calf length "granny" boots.

An idea taken from the gay liberation movement was that stereotyped differences between male and female could be broken down by cross-dressing; this was taken up by women who wanted to make an impression in a man's world. Discarding skirts and high heels in favor of heavy boots and jeans downplayed traditional images of femininity, which were thought to be male-imposed standards of beauty.

Women's executive dress borrowed elements from the suits of their male colleagues, such as men's suiting-type fabrics in subdued colors. For the first time in history, women's pant suits were accepted as stylish city wear. By 1978 padded shoulders and tailored coats were popular, both reflecting the radical feminism of the early seventies and anticipating the power dressing of the yuppie eighties.

The Teenage Gaze

Youth subcultures – their racial identities, styles of dress and behavior, and patterns of consumption, especially in the area of music – were studied by the new wave of sociologists. Interviews and surveys revealed that teenagers, searching for something constant against which to measure themselves, paid an incredible amount of attention to detail when observing the clothing of their peers. American novelist Alison Lurie, with her own acute eye for detail, in 1976 noted that according to junior high school lore "freaks always wear Lees, greasers wear Wranglers, and everyone else wears Levi's."

Skinheads, one type of subculture, grew out of a late sixties British group known as mods, who were a working-class reaction against middle-class hippies. Skinheads were first called all kinds of names: peanuts, skulls, boiled eggs, cropheads. The mods' hair had been cropped to less than half an inch, but the skinhead *crop* was the most severe haircut you could get at the barber. Skinheads looked neat, yet aggressive. They stomped around in tight short trousers (Sta-Prest pants or bleached Levi's), crombies (coats), suspenders, plain or striped Ben Sherman shirts with button-down collars, and big highly polished work boots (Doc Martens) that, to be a real skinhead, had to have eight eyelets. Skinhead girls wore a "feather" haircut, cropped on top with wispy tufts framing the face and neck. (Suedeheads were identifiable by the grown-out crops, sometimes sideburns, and car coats or workmen's jackets.)

Who's on the line? Janet Reger satin underwear represented the top end of the market. This is the sort of suggestive photography that feminists seriously questioned.

Terrorism hit the Paris runways with Daniel Hechter's IRA tweed look for winter 1978–79: black beret and leather jacket, man's shirt with button-down collar and narrow black tie. The roll-down ankle socks worn over stockings were a young woman's fashion inspired by roller-skating gear – but here worn with heavy crêpe-soled, tongued brogues.

Terrorism Strikes

Political protest turned violent, resulting in the hijacking of airplanes and bombing campaigns. The seventies opened with Black September, when four successive hijackings by breakaway Palestinian groups occurred. In 1972 there was Bloody Sunday in Northern Ireland; the massacre of innocent Israelis by Palestinian guerrillas at the Munich Olympic Games; and a car-bombing campaign by the young revolutionary Baader-Meinhof organization in West Germany. Many struggles went on through the decade. 1979 ended with 90 people being held hostage at the American embassy in Iran by military followers of the Ayatollah Khomeini.

Economy Drives

In the early 1970s, the numbers of unemployed and of full-time students rose in the West. By 1975 the world was in recession; unemployment figures had been rising steadily, along with inflation, for a number of years and there was less demand for manufactured goods. The energy crisis of 1973–74 put extra pressure on the manufacturing industry to reduce overhead. By the end of the decade, numbers employed in the fashion-related industries dropped in the West, coinciding with a dramatic decrease in trade union membership; but the number of homeworkers was increasing, especially among the immigrant population. At the same time, recession meant that industry was reluctant to invest in fast-changing technology – it was far cheaper to use Third World labor.

Consequently the global balance shifted as multinational corporations financed from the West manufactured more products in the Far East, taking full advantage of the Free Trade Zones. These areas were centered on ports into which raw materials or component parts could be imported, then assembled and re-exported without paying duties and without complying with trade union agreements and industrial legislations. Women and children were exploited, especially in the clothing and textile industries.

The long-term political and cultural implications were considerable: for the past century, the industrialized West had been treated as the model for developing countries. In its place, Japan entered the vanguard of micro-technology and industrial organization, and prospered.

Divine, the drag performer, with his ultra-blond hair, enjoying the glamour of satin and sparkle.

More Dash Than Cash

As job prospects dwindled, a network of street markets developed for the sale of secondhand clothes. New clothes were made from old. Old and new were worn together, often in unexpected combinations of color, pattern and texture, or of men's and women's clothing. *Cheap Chic*, a guide to "Hundreds of money-saving hints to create your own great look," was a big seller. Its authors declared "Fashion as a dictatorship of the élite is dead."

New aesthetics emerged. Some were achieved with the help of products from the kitchen or bathroom cupboard. People dyed their own T-shirts, sometimes batiking or tie-dyeing them for a late-hippie look. Punk girls dyed their grandfathers' long-johns black; this fashion for leggings developed into the high fashion Lycra versions of the 1980s. The boys customized their hair gels to hold the spikes in place: for the perfect hedgehog, Tony James of the band Generation X used a combination of lemon juice, spit and orange juice: "I used to walk round smelling like a carton of Kia-Ora [orange drink]," he said.

Small Is Beautiful

In unison with the earth's atmosphere, the debates about ecology, appropriate and alternative technology were heating up. Ecology became a political bandwagon: parties like the German Greens and environmental lobby groups like Friends of the Earth and Greenpeace were established. *The Greening of America* (1970), by Yale University law professor Charles Reich, predicted that U.S. society would permanently change for the better because American youth would attach greater importance to conserving the beauty of their environment than to social status and financial success. Prophet of intermediate technology E. F. Schumacher's book *Small Is Beautiful* was published in 1973 and supported by lecture tours and a promotional campaign.

Concern was growing for the endangered animals of the world. Georgina Howell wrote in a 1975 issue of British *Vogue*: "No woman with her eyes open would walk about now in the skins of a rare animal and be the butt of raised eyebrows and uncomplimentary remarks."

Farrah Fawcett, looking like a drum majorette and the picture of American health with her long blonde hair and broad smile.

Black Roots

In 1970, black American tennis player Arthur Ashe was refused a visa to play in the South African championships. The politics of race not only entered the sports arena, but TV and cinema screens too. *Roots*, a televised version of a book by Arthur Hailey, was a U.S. sensation in 1977; the author traced his ancestry to West Africa, in the early days of the slave trade. The program boosted black Americans' sense of cultural identity and inspired many to visit or settle in Africa. Important black images from the 1970s emerged from movies made specifically for black audiences such as Melvin Van Peebles' *Sweet Sweetback's Baadasssss Song* and the *Shaft* films.

Take Care of Yourself

Momentous breakthroughs were taking place in science and medicine. The seventies boasted the first test-tube baby, advances in ultrasound

and in organ transplants. At the same time, interest in alternative medicine was growing; a group of American doctors visited China in 1971 to study acupuncture. In addition, diet and exercise gained an even more prominent place in health care.

Latching onto the cholesterol debate, new ranges of low-fat spreads appeared in the supermarket. Magazines and bookshops were flooded with literature on dieting and food. More people were becoming vegetarians. Fashionable sections of cities now included health food shops and restaurants, and an occasional juice bar.

There was a boom in sportswear and exercise bikes. Many more amateurs ran in marathons; in 1977 and 1978 *The Complete Book of Running* by James F. Fixx was a bestseller in the United States. Health and "natural" good looks were turning into big business. Health clubs were on the increase. They offered swimming pools, saunas, yoga and exercise classes, massage and steam rooms.

Slimming down, by whatever agonizing means, was widespread in the seventies. The woman with the ideal slender figure had no problem burning her bra. At the beginning of the decade, *natural* was a key word in

cosmetics advertising. Estée Lauder launched a range called "Little Nothings." To turn blue eyes greener, brown eyes bluer, or whatever one's fancy was, the latest optical fashion of 1972 was a pair of tinted contact lenses.

Energy Crisis

The Arab oil embargo following the Yom Kippur War of 1973 led to an increase in the price of oil. In the United States, long lines formed at gas stations – if there was any gas at all, for many stations ran out. In Britain the world energy crisis was compounded by a shortage of coal stocks, due to the miners' overtime ban; as a result, industry was restricted to three days' per week electricity supply. Suddenly the power to drive machinery and heat water, as well as to fuel cars and planes, seemed more precious. Oil-based products like synthetic yarns and certain types of plastics increased in price. For economic reasons (environmental advantages were coincidental), the manufacturing and auto industries started to develop energy-saving technologies. Research into solar, wind and geothermal power was stepped up, though unfortunately much of this initiative was abandoned as soon as the oil embargo ended.

Thea Porter's interpretation of exotic eastern dress, with short bolero-jacket and full skirt with paisley motif. These silk and silver clothes were in a class above the casual hippie's Indian block prints and embroidered gauze.

The movie thriller *Shaft*, whose title character was played by Richard Roundtree, was widely known for its theme song.

Colorful kaftans offset by striking rugs of Central Asia at the London men's boutique Hung On You.

Craft Revival

The seventies staged a revitalized interest in crafts such as jewelry, ceramics, hand knitting, embroidery and screen printing on textiles. National and federal councils were set up to promote the crafts, especially those one-of-a-kind items designed and made by art school graduates. New magazines and craft galleries promoted the fine art approach to the fiber arts. They offered an alternative to mass-produced goods; yet at the same time, many craftspeople hoped that their designs might be put into multiple production, thus closing the gap between one-of-a-kind design and industry.

The fashion for handmade clothes and individualistic decoration also applied to the imported traditional and tourist crafts of developing nations of the world, which contributed to the ethnic look of the early seventies.

Jimmy Page of Led Zeppelin, near-naked in soft, clinging satin. The huge flares, cut long and wide around the hem to accommodate platform shoes, made hips and thighs look extra-slim. Hand-painted flowers like these adorned ties, scarves and vests.

The Art Market

Partly due to the alliance between Pop Art and advertising, thanks to Andy Warhol's Factory, the art market became increasingly associated with the promotion of products. Some of the most avant-garde ideas were to be found in advertising photography. They were not so much about what the product looked like, but about the attitude with which it was worn or used.

Some new art forms entered the galleries from the street. Graffiti painting was sprayed or splattered on the sides of subway cars or on walls in the poorer sections of large cities. In New York City, Fab Five Freddy (so-called after the subway line for the number 5 train on which he lived and "worked") became a star performer of the medium. Freddy was also a prophet of 1980s hip-hop, rapping and break dancing.

On the West Coast, rock posters were celebrated in a show held at the San Francisco Museum of Modern Art in 1976. Artists, including David Hockney, Allen Jones, Patrick Hughes and Elizabeth Frink, became involved in T-shirt design, too. Italian knitwear manufacturer Missoni invited painters into their studios, to give a new impetus to fashion.

"Art School," a song about individualism and rebelliousness, was performed by the band The Jam in 1977. Though none of its members had been to art school, many rock musicians had. David Byrne, lead singer of Talking Heads formed in 1975, had studied at the Rhode Island School of Design in Providence. No wonder, then, that there should be direct links between the visual arts and performance, and that some rock music of the period should be influenced by movements in the fine arts.

Human Rights

The struggle for human rights pervaded the world. The message of the politically oppressed was expressed in a variety of ways. In 1970 Alexander Solzhenitsyn's novels addressing the struggles of humans in a repressive political system won him the Nobel Prize for literature. The next year, two films re-evaluating the relations between American Indians and whites were released: *Little Big Man* and *Soldier Blue*. In 1977 Steve Biko, a black trade union leader and a founder of the Black Consciousness Movement, was found dead in a South African police cell. His death provoked major international concern and criticism of the South African regime, as well as a best-selling paperback.

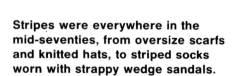

Stripes were everywhere in the mid-seventies, from oversize scarfs and knitted hats, to striped socks worn with strappy wedge sandals.

Yuki's ballooning cape and trousers cut in one, reflecting the Japanese art of draping and folding, and showing off the character of fabric with its striped border and contrasting sections of pattern.

The Music Business

New sounds and musical forms were sometimes a reaction against the conventions of romantic, melodic lyrics. Soul music by performers like J. B. Sly did this. Some music made a deliberate (but artificial) attempt to project the voice of "the people," and so soccer fans' songs were built into the background chorus of British hit songs by Slade and Gary Glitter. Punk singers like Johnny Rotten of The Sex Pistols developed an explicitly working-class voice by using lower-class accents and being deliberately inarticulate. Through the seventies, British bands were drawing inspiration from West Indian ska and reggae music. And new developments in audio technology, notably synthesizers and tape recorders, also contributed to the variety of new beats.

The rock media were beginning to discuss music in the broader context of style. One of the most influential figures in this area was Tom Wolfe, who wrote for America's *Rolling Stone* magazine. British journalists followed his example and argued for more space in the established pop music weeklies *Melody Maker* and *New Musical Express*. Various new magazines appeared: some promoted the popular end of the music business, while others discussed the underground scene and were known as fanzines.

Isaac Hayes and The Emotions – the glamour end of soul. Sometimes black women played down their color, straightened their hair and tinted it with henna. The range of cosmetics specifically for black skins was still limited.

Teeny-bopper sweethearts The Osmonds looked squeaky-clean with their freshly washed hair. Donny was the main attraction, but Jimmy also had his admirers, pictured here with pristine creases in the legs of his zippered white all-in-one suit with embroidered lapels.

The Jackson Five – their lead singer Michael in the center front – wearing Afro hairstyles and a medley of shirts, home-made from women's dress prints, lampshade fringing, and striped furnishing fabric.

By the mid-1970s worldwide music sales grossed well over $4 billion annually – more than film or sports. In *Solid Gold*, a study of the American rock industry, R. Serge Denisoff divided the audience into three groups: young, predominantly female, bubble-gum pop fans (who bought singles and posters to hang on their bedroom walls); older "punk-rockers" (rock as aggressive background music for rituals of dancing, dating and getting stoned at weekends); and collegians ("folk-art-rock" concert-goers and LP listeners, who enjoyed good lyrics).

Teeny-boppers enjoyed The Osmonds, David Cassidy and the tartan-clad Bay City Rollers; sales of their records boomed. The Jackson Five, the group with whom Michael Jackson got his start, were the seventies' biggest selling group on the Motown label.

Success depended on image and performance. The phenomenal international success of the Swedish group Abba was due to their image as well as the new quality of their sound.

New Technology

In 1970 the first microprocessor was patented by Intel, and the first cheap pocket calculators were retailed in the United States. Experiments with tele-shopping began in the seventies. People pondered the dramatic changes of life-style that these advances might bring. Would supermarkets and fashion boutiques soon become institutions of the past? Auto-focus cameras and microchip-programed washing machines were the new "necessities." Matt black digital watches were novel; expensive at first, but thanks to British inventor Clive Sinclair they came down in price, and by the end of the decade Japanese versions were flooding the mass market. The Sony Walkman was launched in 1979. The microprocessor initiated the need for information at one's fingertips; the leather-bound Filofax personal filing system brought it into style.

Fashion Rules OK?

Although it was generally agreed that design added spice to life, real *haute couture* was increasingly being dismissed as anachronistic – "a degenerate institution propped up by a sycophantic press," declared fashion writer Kennedy Fraser in 1975. To survive, established fashion houses like Christian Dior and Yves Saint Laurent were designing more and more ready-to-wear collections and catering to the more casual and practical moods of the moment.

Vogue announced: "There are no rules in the fashion game now." In the early 1970s the magazine featured a vegetable gardener wearing a beret, scarf, wrinkled woolly tights, a loose knitted mohair coat, and commented "the clothes aren't smart, but they're much in fashion."

Nostalgia played a major role through the decade. Walking into the Biba store in London was like stepping back in time. In the dim Art Deco– and Art Nouveau–styled lighting, in between Edwardian lampshades dripping with fringes and huge potted plants reflected in the metallic sheen of the Deco wallpaper and mirrors, you could sink into a plum-colored sofa and wait for a friend. Meanwhile, you watched passers-by try on feather boas, bias-cut scarves, and pull down cloche hats well below the eyebrows until nothing showed but a dark plum-colored mouth.

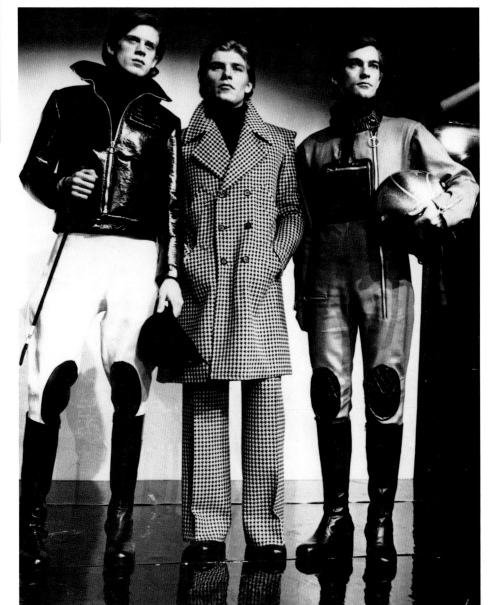

Menswear by Pierre Cardin, 1973–74: functional elements of sports clothing, such as zippers and knee patches, were exaggerated to make bold fashion statements. The black-and-white houndstooth check would usually be made into a jacket or trousers, but never before worn like this.

The boutique culture of the sixties carried on reasonably successfully, though influential shops like Biba in London did not last the decade. However, increasingly the department stores were beginning to fill up with little shops, each devoted to a designer. Henri Bendel of New York was one of the first to do so, in 1970; there were outlets for Thea Porter and Sonia Rykiel clothes.

The revolution in men's fashion retailing took the big stores by storm. Men's boutiques in these big stores sold the latest lines and fabrics. Those that sold internationally found that preferences in menswear varied from one branch to another: lines like navy velvet men's suits sold very well in Paris, but not in London; Frenchmen preferred one center-back vent in the jacket, while the British liked two.

Just as *haute couture* for women was almost a thing of the past, so traditional custom-made tailoring was under threat. Some tailors launched ready-to-wear collections abroad, particularly in Japan.

Tightening the purse strings, so to speak, was necessary for most people in response to the energy crisis and recession. Dedicated followers of fashion with less money to spend were buying more imported clothing, while others opted out and stepped into jeans — leaving the home-grown designers and manufacturers in a vacuum. The rare breed who had cash chose to flaunt it in the luxury of Parisian couture, proving they were immune to financial crises.

Up-and-coming designers began to pave new ways forward. Clovis Ruffin (Ruffinwear) clothes appealed "to the sort of people who are not frightened of pulling things over their hairdos." He used the new generation of silky synthetic jersey fabrics in subtle plain colors: simply constructed, zipperless dresses that could be dressed down or up with plastic or diamonds. Also exploring the aesthetics of new manufacturing technology, Stephen Burrows was the first designer of note to use zig-zag machine-stitching frankly, as structure and decoration.

Members of a London soccer team and models. The men wear the latest fashions by Mr. Freedom, 1973: contrasting lapels and yokes, jeans, "bum-freezer" jackets and stacked heel shoes.

The jet-black hair and Southeast Asian features of this model emerging out of a sea of leopard skins were deliberately chosen for exotic effect.

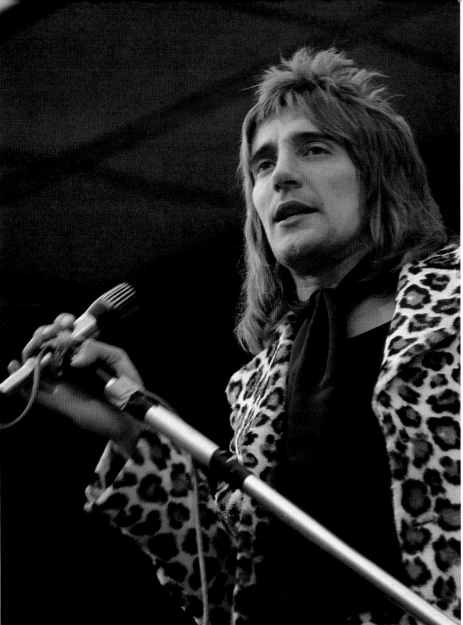

Rod Stewart stalking the stage, his "Rooster" haircut and fake fur jacket worn with tight black T-shirt and casually knotted neckscarf.

Jubilee Year, 1977

Silver Jubilee street parties in Britain celebrated 25 years of Queen Elizabeth's reign on June 7. It was no coincidence that in the same year, purveyors of punk Vivienne Westwood and Malcolm McLaren's shop Sex was renamed Seditionaries, indicating Westwood's belief that people must be *seduced* into revolt. As an anti-Establishment gesture, the "God Save the Queen" T-shirt, featuring Jamie Reid graphics in which a portrait of the queen was defaced, was produced – and banned. Derek Jarman's film *Jubilee* was released in the same year: another chance to shock, and to mix images of conservatism, like a pastel-colored twin sweater set such as the queen might wear, with black leather and rubber.

Rough and Ready

Get Stoned

Left over from the sixties, long hair for men still represented the image of counterculture. While the Establishment may no longer have been shocked by hippie style – with its disheveled appearance suggesting poverty and irresponsibility – it didn't quite trust longhairs either. "Treat this man with respect, he may have just sold a million records" read a framed sign of a downbeat hippie, hanging in the lobby of the Continental Hyatt House hotel on Sunset Boulevard, Los Angeles.

In the United States, The Grateful Dead were the best living monuments to hippie style. In Europe, rich hippies flew to Amsterdam for drugs and to buy long leather coats. Meanwhile London's Kensington Market outfitted hippies with imported Afghan coats, Indian embroidered or printed blouses and floating skirts, and unisex velvet loons (baggy trousers).

It was a body-conscious society. The Rolling Stones' zipper-flyed *Sticky Fingers* album cover of 1971 (designed by Andy Warhol) teased the group's fans about that. Sex, drink and drugs were on everybody's minds; all three were the making and breaking of Jim Morrison, The Doors' lead singer, who died of an alcohol and drug overdose in 1971. His fashion for leather pants lived on for some time.

As ever, leather jackets spelled rough and readiness. They were worn by heavy metal headbangers, whose heroes were hard rock groups like Motörhead, Status Quo and Lynyrd Skynyrd. Denim, daubed with painted images and names of rock icons or encrusted with studs, was an alternative to leather.

Radical Denim

While denim was a kind of uniform, it could also be manipulated or added to, to make a highly individual statement. Levi's jackets were customized with embroidered stars and stripes, super-studded names and messages – one even had an ashtray built into the sleeve!

The traditional blue denim, dyed in indigo, was guaranteed to fade. Fading signified wear and tear and, by implication, hard work. New clothes made from old denim passed as fashion and sold in boutiques at high prices. They included skirts and flared trousers made from jeans by opening up part of the original seam and inserting a triangular gusset.

As well as basic blue, new colors and finishes were introduced, mostly inspired by the worn-out look. Brushed denim simulated the "velvet" feel of an old pair of jeans; colors tended to look drab and washed-out: beige-pink, pale blue, and nondescript tan. Stonewashing – that means what it sounds like, putting new jeans into a pebble-filled washing machine – broke down the even color and starchiness of new cloth. Alternatively, a new pair of jeans was worn in a bath of salty water until it felt skintight. Some dressweight novelty denims were woven with jaunty patterns of teddy bears, flowers and checks.

Denim was even copied in other cloths. Spoofs were printed. In 1972 designer Henry Lehr produced leather suits dyed in denim blue that were much more expensive than the real thing. Gradually a reaction against denim set in; corduroy was a popular alternative for pants and blouson-style jackets.

And so, within the language of denim, there were clear distinctions in terms of how much was spent on any one outfit, or even how you wore and treated your jeans. Rich women walked up New York's stylish Madison Avenue with their well-cut jeans neatly pressed, maybe accessorized by a silk shirt and famous French label scarf, whereas young students might hang out in New York City's Greenwich Village in faded and patched jeans topped with a T-shirt or Indian block-printed cotton blouse.

Lumberjacks and Cowboys Are Alright

A number of stores began to specialize in western styles, selling cowboy boots and other items. The fashion for tucking jeans into boots became part of the seventies' "look." Tooled patterns on rawhide belts were sometimes quite intricate, and just the kind of craft that the hippies of various rural communes made and sold to supplement their vegetable-growing economy.

The tough-guy image implied by wearing lumberjack and cowboy clothes was consciously adopted by the gay community on the West Coast. It was popularized in the later 1970s, when The Village People, a disco squad, dressed up as macho men: cop, construction worker, biker, and cowboy. Versions of this look have persisted as the corporate image of gay fraternity: the handlebar moustache, plaid lumberjack shirt, tight blue jeans, field boots, and a short GI-style cropped haircut.

To writer Tom Wolfe, radical chic meant wearing secondhand "jeans of the people . . . hod carrier jeans . . . at the Army surplus at two pair for twenty-nine cents." The surplus store was also the place to go for camouflage and khaki army fatigues.

An American hippie in London, typified by the long hair, mustache and brushed acrylic jacket; the shoulder-bag holds just enough gear for his life-style on the road.

Bruce Springsteen on his album cover *Darkness on the Edge of Town* looking rough and ready in white T-shirt and black leather jacket, worn with blue jeans.

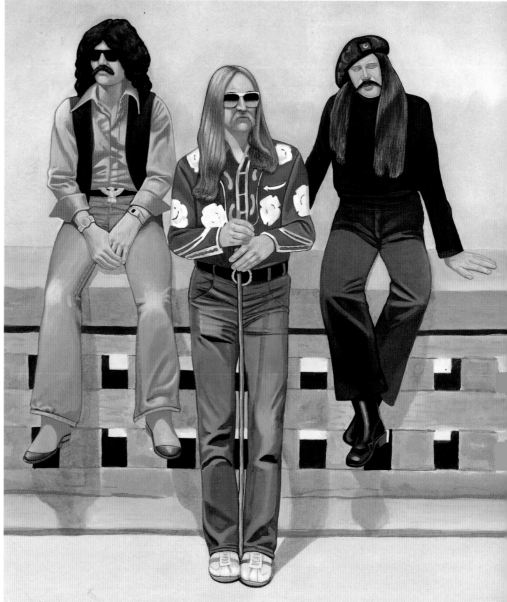

The Doobies looking not much different from on stage – remnants of sixties' psychedelia, long hair, Che Guevara berets and jeans or velvet loons.

Variations on the denim theme: patchwork denim shoulder-bag, wrap-around skirt worn with tight crinkle-cotton shirt, and jeans (now cut for women) tucked into knee-length boots.

Advertisement for Levi's, the essentials of culture. The image is based on the Creation scene painted by Michelangelo on the ceiling of the Sistine Chapel in Rome.

Members of The Village People parodying the most macho images: uniformed air force officers, bikers in black leather gear, cowboys and Indians, and construction workers.

31

Nostalgia

Retro Chic

Secondhand clothes did not have to look sad and drab. They could also be glamorous. The flashier side of thrift-shopping was in San Francisco, where stores like Casey's Faded World dressed up the glitzy members of the transvestite and gay scene. Their style was crystallized by a group called the Cockettes in the early seventies. In London's King's Road, you could walk out of Granny Takes a Trip looking like a Beatle off the *Sergeant Pepper* album cover; the shop sold the distinctive red uniforms of the Chelsea pensioners (retired army personnel from World War I, living just down the road at the Chelsea Hospital), and round gold-rimmed "granny specs," just like those worn by John Lennon.

Rock Back the Clock

Nostalgia was big business. One major influence on the seventies came from the fifties. Elvis, the king of rock, influenced the style and performance of musicians and singers and also captivated the public at large. In 1974 Colin Irwin wrote in *Melody Maker*: "Retailers of soft goods last year sold more than

A combination of ethnic and "granny" elements: the Peruvian poncho knitted in natural cream and brown alpaca wool worn as a skirt, home-made shawl crocheted from odds and ends of colored yarn and soft leather cuffed ankle boots.

$20,000,000 worth of Presley products. . . . Chain, drug and novelty stores now feature lipsticks in autographed cases bearing color names for such Presley hit tunes as Hound Dog Orange, Loving You Fuchsia, and Heartbreak Pink."

Tradition for Sale

There were fashions based on the 1920s, 1930s and 1940s. Period films launched from Hollywood conjured up past styles that were tempting to emulate: these included *The Godfather*

and *The Great Gatsby*. Under the direction of Diana Vreeland, a former editor of American *Vogue*, the Costume Institute at the Metropolitan Museum of Art in New York staged some major exhibitions of costume history, beginning with a retrospective of the Spanish couturier Cristobal Balenciaga.

Of course, although Laura Ashley, Ralph Lauren, punk and new wave fashions all shared elements of nostalgia, there were clearly very different motivations behind their use of the past. And there were obvious differences between authentic secondhand clothes and contemporary designs based on them. Yves Saint Laurent and other Paris designers drew on classic lines from the 1930s and 1940s, using tweeds, crêpes, gabardines and gauzier silks for formal daytime and romantic evening wear. They still had the superb cut and finish expected of *haute couture*.

On the other hand, Laura Ashley made inexpensive printed cotton dresses based on late Victorian and Edwardian styles, featuring ruffles around the neckline and hem, leg-of-mutton sleeves, touches of lace, tucks, buttons and sashes. These had a much less sophisticated look, more rustic, almost like home dressmaking.

The American counterpart of Laura Ashley and Liberty print dresses was Ralph Lauren's "Prairie" look of 1978. Based on the type of dress described in Sears Robuck catalogs of the 1880s, it was typically made of calico or gingham with a ruffled hem, reminiscent of early American settlers' clothing. Lauren's version was worn with layered petticoats. Meanwhile, American preppie and Ivy League styles had become popular in Japan, where the boutiques of Tokyo's Harajuku district sold many reworked versions of traditional British and American looks. Yet for all this nostalgia, wedge shoes and peep-toed sandals echoing wartime ration styles of the 1940s were freshly designed. They grew into platform soles.

Exotica

The traditional clothing of other cultures was another source of inspiration. Paris designer Hanae Mori, who opened a salon in New York in the early 1970s, based many of her de-

signs on the simple shapes and bold decoration of kimono and costume for the traditional Japanese Noh theater. Yves Saint Laurent designed a series of Russian jackets fastened with frogging. The hippies had led a trail not only to India and further east but also to North Africa; the *djellabah*, a Moroccan-type hooded cloak, was the basis for some new coat shapes. Dramatic eastern clothes and textile hangings inspired the kaftan fashion.

Eastern European folk costume inspired the fashion for gauze smocks with embroidered yokes and full sleeves gathered at the wrists. Women wore these with triangular scarves covering their hair and knotted at the back of the neck, known as *babushkas* (meaning "grandmother" in Russian). Men wore red and white printed kerchiefs known as bandannas, or genuine Indian block printed squares, very casually knotted around the neck or around the head, rather like a swashbuckling Hollywood pirate.

German fashion designer Rudolf Mooshamer at Munich Zoo wearing an embroidered *djellabah*; his motto "independence in fashion" incorporated the promotion of dresses for men.

Penelope Tree with Indian-style face paint and suede-thonged armbands and platform sandals decorated with beads. Her dress of elephant crêpe, designed by Walter Albini for Misterfox, was described by an Italian magazine as "maxi-sexy."

A publicity photo for Biba boutique: the backdrop pattern, a blend of Art Nouveau and Art Deco, and subdued coloring resembling a sepia print, conveys an atmosphere of nostalgia.

Yves Saint Laurent took inspiration
from the East – from Romania to
Mongolia – for his collections, taking
advantage of the skilled
embroiderers who distinguished the
Paris *haute couture* industry from
ready-to-wear collections.

Culotte dress. Screen printed fabric
designs were often large in scale;
cheap gilt metal belts were very
popular in the early seventies.

Black Is Beautiful

"Afro" Roots

The Afro hairstyle, symbolizing black culture and "African-ness," began as a countercultural statement, and was then adopted as fashion. Figures like black American rights campaigner Angela Davis were well known for wearing the style.

In 1973, Naomi Sims, a black American model, changed her career and began manufacturing wigs aimed specifically at black women. Each style was given an African name. Three years later, she published a book on black beauty, encouraging black women to be themselves. She wrote: "You do not necessarily have to wear *daishikis* to prove you are proud of being black." Her message echoed the lyrics of James Brown's hit records of the late 1960s: "Say It Loud, I'm Black and I'm Proud." But soon Afro wigs became a white fashion accessory.

Soul Princes

Although the radical chic of white Americans was partially inspired by the Black Panther look, the black street-wise youth of the inner-city slums hardly aspired to looking downbeat. In a time and place where they were closed out of prestigious jobs and restricted from buying or renting houses in "nice" neighborhoods, cars and clothes became status symbols. For them, the style of stars like James Brown, Nancy Wilson and Diana Ross, who had made the international charts and in the process had achieved great financial success, was most influential. The James Brown look had nothing to do with army fatigues, and everything to do with ruffled shirts, black-belted leather pieces and bell-bottom herringbones.

Tom Wolfe described the black "soul princes" of New Haven Connecticut's Dixwell Avenue who aspired to funky chic: ". . . wearing their two-tone patent Pyramids with the five-inch heels that swell out at the bottom to match the Pierre Chareau Art Deco plaid bell-bottom baggies they have on with the three-inch-deep elephant cuffs tapering upward toward the 'spray-can fit' in the seat . . . and the black Pimpmobile hat with the four-inch turn-down brim and the six-inch pop-up crown with the golden chain-belt hatband . . ."

James Brown, whose image was one of the most potent influences on fashionable black American youth.

Caribbean Culture

In the seventies, West Indian culture made its presence felt on style and performance in a number of ways. On one hand, there was the exuberance of carnival; the other face of black style was cool, lingering in the shadows, a style cultivated in the 1960s from the American ''soul-brother'' image: a loose-limbed black figure in tight-fitting gear, moving to the off-beat of jazz, ska and rhythm and blues.

When it came to style, the Rastafarian movement's religious roots became obscured in reggae music. Rastafarians are members of a West Indian, particularly Jamaican, group that rejects Western culture and regards Haile Selassie, the emperor of Ethiopia overthrown by a military coup in 1974, as divine. As for style, Rastas were recognized by their dreadlocks of long, plaited hair, and the colors of the Ethiopian flag — red, green and gold. These were deeply symbolic because the accession of Haile Selassie to the Ethiopian throne in 1930 pointed to the imminent downfall of white colonialism — and to the liberation of black peoples. Various items of dress were decorated in the three colors: buttons, cardigans, shirts, sandals, tams (knitted or crocheted woolen hats) and walking sticks.

Northern Soul

American soul music exported to Europe and sold through specialist record shops developed various distinctive, if obscure, cult followings. They turned American soul upside down and inside out, into something quite un-American that created a new chapter in the history of subcultures.

In 1972, a short-lived cult, northern soul, centered on the North of England clubs like the Wigan Casino. It was a truly underground, secret activity, involving working-class kids in a life of all-night dancing. The jerky rhythms of the solo dance acts, pumped up by amphetamines (pills were very much part of the cult), broke into incredible back flips, hand springs, and mid-air whirls. These soul dancers had close-cropped hair, clinging vests, madly flapping wide trousers, and buttons with slogans like ''Keep the Faith.''

Free Your Mind and Your Ass Will Follow, **Funkadelic's album cover of 1970.**

Fresh album cover featuring J. B. Sly.

Funky chic flaunted by New York
dudes Graham Central Station on
their album cover.

The Afro hairstyle entered the white
fashion agenda – here, members of
the band Santana, early exponents of
world music.

Bob Marley, one of the greatest reggae musicians, wearing a knitted vest in the colors of the Ethiopian flag and dreadlocks – symbols of Rastafarianism.

Donna Summer, one of the most romantic and glamorous black American singers.

Diana Ross and her back-up vocalists, looking like something out of the popular sci-fi TV series *Star Trek*.

Glamour

Glam Rock

The term *glam rock* refers to seventies rock performance that built pure glamour into the act. Bryan Ferry and Roxy Music, David Bowie, Rod Stewart, Marc Bolan and Elton John are the best known "glam rockers." Beneath the sparkling surface, there were undercurrents of sexual innuendo, ranging from the outright campiness of the cult film *The Rocky Horror Picture Show* (1972) to the artful seduction of Roxy Music. (The name Roxy is derived from "Rock Sexy.")

As the more successful rock stars got richer, and more glamorous, so their fantasies built up into an ominous sense of stage power. Making the dress and the act more glamorous seemed to bridge the gap between rock and pop. Style carried a high price – and reaped generous rewards in the spin-offs from records.

Right at the beginning of the decade, Roxy Music's album covers married women's fashion with male rock performance. On the *For Your Pleasure* cover, model Amanda Lear offered a look-but-don't-touch kind of image, as if she had just stepped out of some high society portrait. The man behind Roxy Music's dress style was London designer Antony Price.

David Bowie

The most successfully packaged glam rock star was David Bowie – better known to some as Ziggy Stardust, though that was only one of a rapidly shifting sequence of personalities, looks and stage sets. He hit the album charts with a series of five LPs between 1971 and 1974. No sooner did fans copy the original Ziggy haircut than Bowie was onto the next interpretation of it, on the *Aladdin Sane* album of 1973. By then, in the UK there were plenty of Ziggy boys and girls standing at bus stops and hanging about pop record stores, waiting for the next Bowie album. Their hair was dyed green or orange, their eyelids brushed with glitter.

Healthy glamour, with plastic visor, bra-top and tight shiny zippered jacket and pants.

The definitive Ziggy haircut made the hair stand on end like a little red rooster, with a puffball in front and razored into the nape of the neck behind. The "Rooster," and the longer "Shag" version, were taken up by other stars, including Gary Glitter and Rod Stewart.

Bowie's disguise was a cover-up for his shyness. The look was calculatedly androgynous and artificial. What he was doing was the exact opposite of what the feminists were aiming for; they were playing down appearance, rejecting glamour. But Bowie and other stars flaunted it.

All that Glitters

Though some other male rock stars toyed with the androgynous look, others followed the overt sexuality of heavy metal Led Zeppelin's lead singer Robert Plant. But even the most macho of acts in the early seventies could not ignore the power of glamour. Hobnail boots were decorated with silver nailheads and made with high heels. Freddy Mercury of Queen had stage wear designed by Zandra Rhodes. Slade decked themselves in satin, adjusting their image to the mood of the moment, but not actually initiating a style.

Female glam rockers like Suzi Quatro were just as theatrical, though there was no hint of drag. Nona Hendryx of Labelle was one of the most glamorous. Her image was created by two American designers, Larry LeGaspi and Norma Kamali. LeGaspi enjoyed playing with shock tactics, inspired by space suits. The Martian look was helped by details of padding and quilt-

ing; these were combined with slinky fabrics and a body-stocking fit. The use of plumage hinted at the fantasy worlds of the Ziegfeld Follies and Busby Berkeley. Costume jewelry, designed by Richard Erker, completed the outfit.

Two other big-time female stage performers were American Chrissie Hynde of the British group The Pretenders, and Pat Benatar of the United States. Unlike Labelle, they modeled their costume on male rock stars. Hynde put together unexpected combinations of hard and soft gear, ruffles with leather, or lace gloves with a cutdown worn denim jacket: her models were the foppish sixties group The Kinks and Robert Plant. Pat Benatar, on the other hand, combined discostyle spandex outfits and stiletto heels with macho metaphors drawn from heavy metal performance.

Marc Bolan, whose lurex stage clothing was based on the gold suit of his idol Elvis Presley. His "Les Paul" guitar, made by Gibson, was one of the most famous sounds of early seventies heavy metal and blues music, though its design dates from the 1950s.

Cork made platform shoes lighter to get around in, and the ankle strap was essential to hold the shoe intact: even so, this was hardly safety gear for biking.

Glitter make-up for parties and on stage: here, sequins have been sewn onto skin-hugging tops of transparent net.

Nona Hendryx of Labelle, dressed in silvery-white, inspired by astronauts' clothing. The body stocking, quilting and padding were elements of the fashion collections of Norma Kamali and Larry LeGaspi, the two designers behind Labelle's glamorous stage presence.

David Bowie, with his Ziggy haircut dyed the hottest shade of red; the slinky asymmetry of the body stocking and feather boa created a deliberately ambiguous, androgynous image.

Dressed to Clash

Like Hell!

Possibly the most lasting image of the seventies has been punk. In 1976–77 the media paid so much attention to it that punk has overshadowed the original American rock stage acts from which many elements of the style came. In early 1975, John Lydon (a.k.a. Johnny Rotten) adopted the short, spiky haircut that is associated with punk; he had seen it in a photo of New York art band singer Richard Hell, who had invented the style in 1974. The New York Dolls and The Ramones (who wore jeans deliberately torn just below the knee) were very influential. Television wore their hair short in direct contrast to the hippies.

Many groups went even further than wild hairstyles. Stage performances often caused controversy. Alice Cooper, for instance, worked simulated killings into his performances of 1972. But possibly the most individual act was The Tubes', from America's West Coast. In their stage show the leader, Fee Waybill, wore metal-studded leather and an executioner's mask-helmet. His female assistant, Re Styles, was flung about the stage, wearing a black leather head-gagger, corset and strappy high-heeled shoes.

By 1977, the Mohican hairstyle, or Mohawk, taken from the Mohawk Indians, had become an identifying feature of punk youths. The cut was worn by Robert de Niro, starring as Travis Bickle in Martin Scorsese's 1976 film *Taxi Driver*. The Mohawk looked down-beat, signifying the spiral down which Bickle was about to slide; but in 1945 it had been a symbol of good luck worn by U.S. paratroopers. A vital aspect of the shock tactic was

the overturning of contexts, giving new meaning to old ideas.

Seditionaries

Punk may have begun in New York, but it was cleverly capitalized on in London by Malcolm McLaren and his partner Vivienne Westwood. They sold "bondage trousers" (with the legs strapped together behind the knees) at their World's End shop. Their clothes reflected the political argument that punk was somehow countercultural and rooted in the working classes.

Though often described as knowingly anarchic, the punk style was more often a meaningless assemblage of dog-collars, safety pins, zippers, chains, school blazers, leather skirts and ripped and torn shirts. The look was widely known through album covers, posters, live performance of songs like The Sex Pistols' *Anarchy in the UK* and fanzines like *Sniffin' Glue*.

Priestesses of Punk

Punk is arguably one youth culture and style that has involved women in a major way. There were a number of influential figures from the American rock scene: rock poet Patti Smith, for instance, who wore layer upon layer of cardigans, men's shirts, ties and big jackets, all of different lengths. Another look of hers included a loose-fitting, frumpish dress worn with heavy unlaced workboots. She modeled her look on the clothes and

attitude of male rock heroes, especially Keith Richards of The Rolling Stones, Bob Dylan, Jim Morrison, and Jimi Hendrix, and on the French poet Rimbaud.

Another American, Debbie Harry (the lead singer of Blondie), created a sensation early in her career through shock gimmicks in her stage act. She appeared in a New York nightclub wearing a white wedding dress, and then ripped it off while belting out *Rip Her to Shreds*.

Acts Lene Lovich and The Slits put outfits together from thrift-shops, almost as if they were little girls playing dress-up, putting together tutus and Wellington boots and badly applying their make-up.

More sixties cast-offs like skinny-rib sweaters and shift dresses, and aggressively hard, shiny synthetic fabrics, were adopted by Fay Fife of the Rezillos, Pauline of Penetration, and Poly Styrene of X-Ray Spex. Ski pants or fishnet stockings completed some outfits. These band members asserted their sexual freedom and poked fun at the radical feminists' denouncement of fashion, while the B-52's played on a fifties cocktail-drinking society with their enormous wigs and secondhand glamour dresses.

The Clash, neatened up to look new wave.

Poly Styrene of X-Ray Spex, subverting the conservatism of pastel-colored suits; the lurex texture adds a hint of bad taste, while the cleaning lady scarf is a defiant anti-glamour gesture. She flaunts the ultimate designer label: an OXFAM ticket pinned to one lapel.

The New York Dolls playing around with gender and trying a few shock tactics, wearing make-up, women's blouses and high-heeled soft leather thigh boots.

Trash Culture

Cut out the Garbage

Designers of new jewelry began turning away from materials like precious metals and semiprecious stones, and instead using cheap materials, like nylon filament and acrylics, experimentally. They were focusing on the design concept: new forms and meanings, and a celebration of bright color.

There were several reasons for this "trash culture." The latest technological breakthroughs in polymer science made available new kinds of plastic, which were much easier to manipulate and more wearable than they had been in the sixties. And built into them were new textures, weights, color effects. There was also an element of shock value in using cheap and cheerful substances, which were conventionally associated with bad taste, and

low or popular culture. And then there was the economic argument. With the seventies recession, designers had little money to invest in expensive materials — and although the buying public was hungry for novelty, people had limited funds. Fashion, too, played a big part. Synthetic jewelry was the obvious accessory to artificial, day-glo hair colors.

By 1977, the spirit of nihilism, a rejection of current beliefs, and the influence of kitsch, as self-conscious bad taste, had filtered through the art colleges and into the fashion industry. Safety pins were used as jewelry. Brown parcel paper was cut out, varnished and manipulated into hair ornaments, brooches and sophisticated handbags. Toolboxes were used as handbags. Regular readers of *Cosmopolitan* magazine sent in for the *Cosmo* clutch bag special offer: a cheap handbag, made of garish plastic, looking like a folded copy of the magazine itself.

Unlimited editions of Pop Art printed on Parisian men's jackets.

Pinball Wizardry

The technicolor world of *The Wizard of Oz* came alive in the zany, fun stage outfits of Elton John. His all-in-one suits of satin or brightly knitted material were decorated with cut-out stars and pom-poms. These were worn with platform boots in a jigsaw of colors and shapes, sufficiently outrageous for walking down "The Yellow Brick Road." He was a singing, dancing, jumping pinball machine come to life! His eyeballs rolled within the frames of his glasses, some of which were illuminated by miniature flashing lightbulbs.

Plastic jeans, padded satin jackets with crass images in embroidery or appliqué, and lime green lurex 12-inch platform shoes: these were all part of the fun of hideous seventies "style." Reactions have induced such revulsion, that most of the "trash culture" has been chucked into the garbage can, rather than be kept for museums of art and design.

But as well as the garish, affordable end of this style, there were toned-down versions, especially in footwear. Classics included Chelsea Cobbler platform sandals decorated with bright-colored leather roses and Yves Saint Laurent rope-sole wedge espadrilles in primary colors, laced up the calf over tights of brightly clashing colors. The shoe designs of Manolo Blahnik and Maud Frizon showed how witty and innovative the unexpected mixture of materials could be: both highly original, and yet very much the spirit of the seventies.

The Fiorucci Phenomenon

An Italian wizard who transformed the images of Pop Art and American graffiti into a highly successful retail business was Elio Fiorucci. Street culture is what he drew on. Fiorucci jeans of corduroy presented a bright spectrum of color that made the earlier seventies brushed denim and Levi's 501s look very drab indeed. Pockets were brashly zipped up with gold metal, and decorated with printed plastic tags, and pink T-shirts printed with red, blue and green and bright yellow stars, or orange T-shirts printed with scarlet roses were fixed at the neck with woven lurex "Fiorucci" labels.

This transfer-printed and airbrushed style was also applied to highly individualistic painted clothing and accessories such as belts and ties. The graphics of T-shirts also carried messages, using the language of popular culture, or nonsensical splashes of sound-words picked out of comic-strip balloons, as in a Roy Lichtenstein canvas or Richard Hamilton collage of the late 1960s.

"Fun suits" for 1977 in man-made fibers. The man in the center wears pants in Terylene/cotton, with a T-shirt in nylon jersey. The overalls and vest and the jacket and shorts worn by the women are also made in nylon.

Bright colors and plastic finishes for overalls and parkas designed by Daniel Hechter for winter 1978–79.

Fiorucci used striking images for its advertising campaigns in the 1970s. Here skin-tight pants are worn by topless models.

Caroline Broadhead was a leading figure of the new generation of designer-craftspeople who used synthetic materials to make affordable fashion accessories.

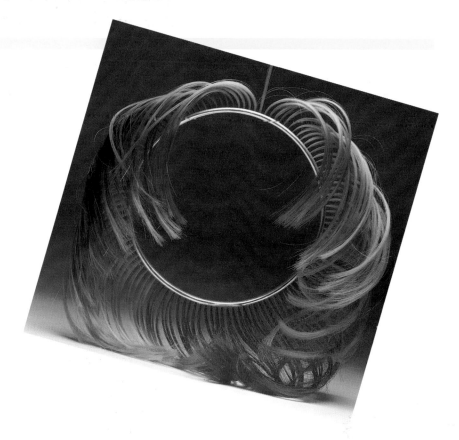

Elton John had a wardrobe of glitter bodysuits and colored glasses to go with them; this jacket was modeled on a circus ringmaster's tailcoat.

Many seventies clothes were far from flattering: here, a knitted bodysuit with grimacing face, and quilted and appliqué hot pant suit.

Disco Kings and Queens

Body Stockings

The summer of 1970 was coined by the newspapers "the nudest ever." But the tiny bikinis and swimsuits of that year were nothing compared with exaggeratedly high legs of 1976 or minimal swimsuits like the "String," the "Savage" and the "Thong," promoted by Los Angeles–based Rudi Gernreich, who was designing Lycra bodywear for the French firm Lily.

The idea was to appear as if your body had been spray-painted. This impression was created by the new ranges of leotards, worn for working out in the gym, for playing ball on the beach or for bopping at the disco. One of the most innovative and successful manufacturers of leotards was Danskin, which made a whole range of coordinating bodywear, leotards with contrasting tights and wrap-around skirts.

For disco dancewear young women wore leotards with all kinds of decoration: short frilled skirts, cap sleeves, spots, stripes and rhinestones. These were also the "in" gear for exercise, and for ice skating. They were sometimes worn with leg warmers – a feature that began with warming up in the gym or in the dance studio and ended up as a fashion statement.

Hot pants were big news in the early seventies. They were extra skimpy shorts. Fashion writer of the *New Yorker* Kennedy Fraser noted: "Satin shorts are vulgar. Knitted shorts are nice, and crocheted shorts are delightful, but both are hard to wear." Hot pants of leather, suede and velvet were generally considered OK and had the advantage of softening, once worn in.

It was the new generation of designers who created "fun" clothing – for teenagers. This included Americans Bill Blass and Geoffrey Beene. Youthful optimism was expressed in color, for this was one way to stand out from the established designers and older generations: yellow shorts next to purple tights, worn with orange platforms. But whether the hemline was maxi or mini, women of any age could indulge in a pair of colorful striped tights or over-the-knee socks – preferably clashing with the feet, whether scarlet workboots, emerald green square-toed sandals or fuschia ankle-boots.

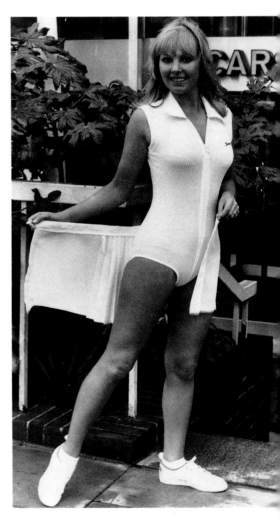

The new range in tennis wear by Slazenger for 1974: a zip-up bodysuit with kilt-style wrap-around skirt.

Jogging Along

As jogging became a popular pastime, so tracksuits were manufactured in a wide range of colors. Coordinated headbands, frequently striped, were very popular. This sportswear began to influence daytime clothing and disco- and party-wear. In fact, the whole of fashion reflected the more informal life-style and behavior. This sense of ease was brilliantly expressed under the Williwear label, designed by American Willi Smith.

More and more sports stars were turning professional, and this put commercial pressure on the business of sportswear design. A whole new heraldry emerged through the symbolism of sneaker logos. Sports shoes developed marks like the Nike wave, Converse star, the Adidas triple stripe, or the Puma flying wedge. Status was endorsed not by a label with the designer's name but by the sports star who promoted it.

Roller Coasting

In around 1978, in hot pursuit of the skateboarding craze, roller skating and roller disco flashed onto the scene. Lycra and other stretchy, shiny fabrics were especially appropriate for these sports. Fashion designers were quick to latch onto the act, producing a range of clothes to complement the skates. One example included a pale pink satin vest (resembling a loose camisole), boxer shorts, and fuschia pink leather skating boots; worn with the now obligatory headband.

Saturday Night Fever

The 1977 film *Saturday Night Fever* brought John Travolta into the limelight and put disco on the map. Travolta played the dance-loving Brooklyn hardware store assistant Tony Manero. The story was based on *Another Saturday Night*, an article written by rock and pop chronicler Nik Cohn for *New York Magazine*. In his story, 2001 Odyssey is "the only disco in all Bay Ridge [Brooklyn] that truly counted." To qualify as one of the faces seen there: ". . . an aspirant need only be Italian, between the ages of eighteen and twenty-one, with a minimum stock of six floral shirts, four pairs of tight trousers, two pairs of Gucci-style loafers, two pairs of platforms, either a pendant or a ring, and one item in gold."

The formula was magic: it was followed by a spate of feverish discomania, and Travolta's sequel film *Grease*. Among the spin-offs were T-shirts and posters.

The roller-skating and skate-boarding crazes sparked new fashion ideas. Denise Crosby (left), granddaughter of singer Bing, and friend Candy Moore, modeling designs by Marion Kops. Denise said "I just love this outfit – it's a gas: so space-orientated."

Norman Parkinson photo of model wearing leotard with matching candlewick cotton jacket and contrasting belt to draw attention to her slim waist.

John Travolta, disco dancing star of the film *Saturday Night Fever*. Millions of screaming fans adopted the beat, if not the look; and hair gel came back in fashion in a big way.

Jane Fonda's lean routine brought fun fitness into the living room, via the television screen, and though the widespread marketing of records and videocassettes of her fast-moving workout program.

Exercise was a new, but lasting fad of the seventies, bringing fashion and sport closer than ever: underwear, sleepwear, hot pants, striped socks and headbands were all coordinated.

The Rebirth of Style

Designer Labels

Early in the decade Pierre Cardin, in whom so much faith had been put during the 1960s, was already being criticized for over-selling the franchise of his name. Other designers lost prestige by attaching their names to anything from suitcases to sheets.

Halston was one of America's first celebrity designers. Having outfitted Jackie Kennedy with her famous pillbox hats and clothed celebrities like Lauren Bacall, Liza Minnelli and Bianca Jagger, in 1973 he signed a deal with Norton Simon Inc., which purchased the right to use Halston's name on any product. This led to the launch of Max Factor's Halston scent.

The story was very different for newcomers to the designer label game. In 1978 Hirsch, the Manhattan entrepreneur behind Hong Kong jeans manufacturer Murjani, persuaded American socialite Gloria Vanderbilt to be photographed wearing jeans bearing her signature on a back pocket. The effect was instantaneous: in the first year, Murjani's sales multiplied sixfold. Women had grown tired of unisex, which made no allowances for curvy hips and concave waistlines. Vanderbilt persuaded women of the virtues of those designs dubbed with her name: "You don't have to lie on the floor to zip up my slacks, yet they are so constructed so they don't gape at the back."

In order to justify costing double or triple the price of regular jeans, designer jeans stood out from the rest of the crowd by the subtlest and least practical of details: back pockets were omitted and quadruple seams introduced. But the greatest distinction was the designer's name fixed to the visible label. Calvin Klein and Pierre Cardin joined the designer-jeans rat race, and Italian manufacturers were quick to produce cheaper versions, aimed at a younger market.

Bill Gibb halterneck dress and matching jacket, made from a printed textile inspired by computer graphics.

Back to the Classics

Following the 1973 oil crisis, men and women alike were economizing and investing in good-quality classics. Some of the famous ready-to-wear figures such as Jean Muir, Sonia Rykiel, Diane Von Fürstenberg and Karl Lagerfeld of the Chloé boutique, succeeded in producing simple, timeless shapes inspired by classical drapery, which were nevertheless extremely difficult to imitate. Naturally, the key to distinction was the quality and fiber of the cloth; this justified the expense of even the simplest cut of top designer-made clothes.

By the mid-seventies relative newcomers to the ready-to-wear scene, from America, Italy and Japan, and to a lesser extent Britain, Germany and Scandinavia, challenged the status quo and Paris couture with a more relaxed attitude to cut and construction. Newcomers to Paris included: Issey Miyake, Yohji Yamamoto, Kansai Yamamoto, Rei Kawakubo of Comme des Garçons, Joseph Ettegui, and Kenzo of Jungle Jap.

Unstructured Elegance

In 1974 the focus on contemporary design moved away from a formal view of clothes – neat, stiffly structured suits, and smart dresses with restaurant-length hemlines – toward a much softer "unconstructed" mode. The concept involved the simplest cuts – deceptively looking as if no skillful cutting was required. Increasingly, the unstructured look depended on the built-in drape and handle of jersey cloths, which could be made up quickly and economically but which would emulate the sophistication, body-cling and swirl of the pre–World War II bias cut. These garments showed off the body, were easy to wear and live in – but they also possessed style.

The mid-seventies pioneer of the unstructured jacket was Giorgio Armani of Milan, who set up his own business as design consultant in 1975, and soon began manufacturing his own ready-to-wear label. Armani's shoulders had a hard-edged, authoritative, executive width. No wonder Armani has often been described as the champion of women's power-dressing, beginning in the seventies. That apparently loose elegance, though in a more comic, relaxed form, was created by Ralph Lauren and modeled by Diane Keaton in the film *Annie Hall* (1977).

In fact, the suit was to become the name of the game in the 1980s for all men and women who were determined to get ahead.

Issey Miyake's wool cowboy look for winter 1978–79; a good example of the seventies experimentation in textured knitting.

Calvin Klein's tomato red linen jacket, white silk crêpe blouse and soft leather pants with elasticized waist and seams at the knee, featured in *Vogue* 1979.

Classic elegance from Jean Muir in this flowing red dress, which appeared in the 1970s.

An elegant but practical line of the late 1970s by Karl Lagerfeld, who designed under the Chloé label. An interest in pliable knitted textures, garments constructed from few pieces, and off-beat colors were typical of the decade.

Glossary

Armani, Giorgio (b. 1935) Italian designer. In the 1960s he worked for menswear manufacturer Nino Cerruti. Set up own consultancy in 1975; worked for several companies, including Emanuel Ungaro, before establishing Armani fashion label.

Ashley, Laura (1925–85) British designer and manufacturer, with company based in Wales; shops opened worldwide in 1970s. Produced Victorian and Edwardian-style dresses of printed cottons with a country look.

Beene, Geoffrey (b. 1927) American designer trained in United States and Paris. Began ready-to-wear in 1963; less expensive line called "Beene Bag."

Biba, mail-order business set up in 1963 by Barbara Hulanicki; soon developed into London's Biba boutique; in 1973 it took over Art Deco department store in London; known for nostalgic, moody clothes.

Blass, Bill (b. 1922) American designer of sportswear whose practical approach to fashion permeates his softer, more luxurious evening garments.

Cardin, Pierre (b. 1922) French designer who worked for Paquin, Schiaparelli and Dior before launching his first womenswear collection in 1957, followed in 1963 by ready-to-wear. During the 1970s Cardin expanded the franchise aspect of his name and business.

Djellabah Hooded cloak with wide sleeves, of Moroccan origin.

Fiorucci, Elio (b. 1935) Italian designer and retailer who established his own house in the 1960s but best known in the 1970s for bright, fun clothing, including slimfit jeans, sold internationally at Fiorucci boutiques.

Gibb, Bill (b. 1943) A British designer, he set up his own company in 1972, with retail business from 1975; known for evening dresses in floaty and exotic fabrics, sometimes with appliqué or embroidery.

Halston (1932–1990) American milliner turned clothing designer who dressed Jackie Kennedy from the 1960s and created simple ready-to-wear knitwear and elegant sportsclothes of jersey fabrics through 1970s. One of the first big American names to franchise his label.

Hechter, Daniel (b. 1938) French designer; known for rain-, duffle- and greatcoats with a difference (e.g., made of jersey), sporty blazers and divided skirts.

Johnson, Betsey (b. 1942) American designer who created extravagant disco wear in the 1970s. She opened her own sportswear business in 1978.

Kamali, Norma (b. 1945) American designer known for cheerleader skirts, glamorous bodysuits and easy, extra-light coats and suits, using industrial and active sports fabrics like parachute nylon and sweatshirting.

Mori, Hanae (b. 1926) Japanese designer. She opened a New York salon in the early 1970s. In 1977 she showed her first couture collection in Paris; design ideas influenced by traditional Japanese kimono and obi (sash).

Muir, Jean (c. 1935) British designer of classic clothes made of heavyweight rayon jerseys and punched and stitched suede.

Porter, Thea (b. 1927) British. In the 1960s she sold antique Near Eastern textiles from London shop and began designing "ethnic" clothes from exotic fabrics for evening wear. She opened a store in New York in 1968, and one in Paris in the early 1970s.

Price, Antony (b. 1945) British. His designs for Bryan Ferry and Roxy Music led to success by mid-1970s; in 1979 he launched his own label.

Rykiel, Sonia (b. 1930) French designer; known in the 1970s mostly for knitwear, in subtle colors of beige, gray and slate blue.

Saint Laurent, Yves (b. 1936) French. Former chief designer at Dior, in 1962 he set up his own house. In the 1970s he designed impeccably cut suits: some inspired by exotic Eastern and Russian sources, some more sober for the new executive woman.

Smith, Willi (1948–1991) American designer of ethnic influenced sportswear inspired by trips to India. He set up Willi Wear casual sportswear in 1976.

Von Fürstenberg, Diane (b. 1946) Belgian born, in 1968 she apprenticed to Italian textile manufacturer Angelo Ferretti and opened her own business in New York in 1972. Known for plain, simply cut or wrap printed silk jersey dresses.

Kawakubo, Rei (b. 1942) Japanese designer behind Comme des Garçons, formed in 1969. Favors somber colors and deliberately disheveled, draped clothes in reaction against traditional ideas of femininity.

Kenzo (b. 1940) Japanese designer, born Kenzo Takada. In the 1960s in Paris he was a freelance designer for Louis Feraud. In 1970 he opened his own Jungle Jap shop. He is known for dynamic layers and mixtures of patterns and bright colors, inspired by traditional and folk dress.

Klein, Calvin (b. 1942) American designer. After working for New York manufacturers of coats and suits, in 1968 he set up his own sportswear business. During the 1970s his designs became increasingly sophisticated; sleek lines and soft and crisp fabrics of silk, linen and fine suede.

Lagerfeld, Karl (b. 1938) German born, but career based in Paris, designed free-lance for Krizia, Charles Jourdan and Fendi; through the 1970s he was particularly associated with Chloé ready-to-wear collections.

Lauren, Ralph (b. 1939) American designer. Worked for Brooks Brothers, then Beau Brummel neckwear. In 1968 he launched the Polo line of menswear; from 1971 he did womenswear collections, including designer jeans and in 1978 the "Prairie" look.

Missoni Italian family-run company founded 1953; raised profile of knitwear in 1970s through boldly patterned long cardigans and sophisticated sweaters for men and women.

Miyake, Issey (b. 1935) Japanese designer. Studied fashion in Paris; worked for Guy Laroche, Hubert de Givenchy and Geoffrey Beene. Held first fashion show in New York, 1971; the next in Paris, 1973.

Yuki (b. 1937) Japanese designer, born Gnyuki Torimaru. Worked for Louis Feraud, Norman Hartnell and Pierre Cardin before designing collections under his own name from 1973. In 1970s he designed one-size jersey dresses of tubes and rectangles, made fluid through draping and the movement of the body.

Reading List

A great deal has been written and published about the 1970s – this reading list is only a very small selection. Magazines and movies of the period are another excellent source of information.

Berger, J., *Ways of Seeing* (BBC Publications, 1972).

Campling, E., *Portrait of a Decade: The 1970s* (Batsford, 1989).

de Marly, D., *Fashion for Men* (Batsford, 1985).

Evans, C. and Thornton, M., *Women and Fashion* (Quartet Books, 1989).

Fraser, K., *The Fashionable Mind* (Alfred A. Knopf, 1989).

Frith, S., *Sound Effects: Youth, Leisure, and the Politics of Rock* (Constable, 1983).

Greer, Germaine, *The Female Eunuch* (McGraw-Hill Publishing Co., 1971).

Hebdige, D., *Subculture: The Meaning of Style* (Methuen, 1979).

Henley, N. M., *Body Politics* (Prentice Hall, 1977).

Hodges, M., *Britain in the 1970s* (Batsford, 1989).

Jones, D., *Haircults* (Thames & Hudson, 1990).

Koren, L., *New Fashion Japan* (Kodansha International, 1984).

McDermott, C., *Street Style* (The Design Council, 1987).

McRobbie, A. (ed.), *Zoot Suits and Second-Hand Dresses* (Macmillan Education, 1989).

Milinaire, C. and Troy, C., *Cheap Chic* (Outlet Book Company, 1976).

Papenek, V., *Design for the Real World: Human Ecology and Social Changes* (Pantheon Books, 1971).

Polhemus, T. and Procter, L., *Fashion and Anti-Fashion* (Thames & Hudson, 1978).

Savage, J., *England's Dreaming: The Sex Pistols and Punk Rock* (Faber, 1991).

Stewart, T. (ed.), *Cool Cats: 25 Years of Rock 'N' Roll Style* (Eel Pie Publishing, 1981).

Tomerlin Lee, S. (ed.), *American Fashion* (André Deutsch, 1976).

Walker, J. A., *Cross-Overs: Art into Pop/Pop into Art* (Methuen, 1987).

Wilson, E. and Taylor, L., *Through the Looking Glass* (BBC Books, 1989).

Wolfe, T., *Mauve Gloves & Madmen, Clutter & Vine* (Farrar, Strauss & Giroux, 1976).

Wolfe, T., *Radical Chic & Mau & Mauing the Flak Catchers* (Bantam Books, 1971).

Acknowledgments

The Author and Publishers would like to thank the following for permission to reproduce illustrations: B. T. Batsford for page 12; BFI Stills, Posters and Designs for pages 6 and 16; Caroline Broadhead for page 51a; Camera Press for pages 11, 26, 34a, 35b and 54b; The Hulton Picture Company for pages 8b, 9, 17, 20, 21, 24, 25, 29, 32, 33, 40, 41, 49, 52, 53 and 56; David Redfern for page 38; Rex Features for the frontispiece and pages 7, 8a, 13, 14, 15, 18, 19, 22a, 22b, 23, 27, 30c, 31a, 36–37, 39b, 39c, 42a, 42c, 43b, 45b, 47a, 47b, 47c, 48, 48–49, 50a, 51b, 55a, 57 and 63. The illustrations were researched by David Pratt.

Time Chart

NEWS	EVENTS	FASHIONS

70

U.S. invades Cambodia
Four students at Kent State University in Ohio are killed by National Guard troops during antiwar protest
U.S. celebrates the first Earth Day
Five planes are hijacked by Black September Palestinian guerrillas
Civil war erupts in Jordan

Isle of Wight festival "of music and love" opens in Britain: Jimi Hendrix gives last public appearance
American film *M*A*S*H*, starring Donald Sutherland and Elliot Gould, premieres
First cheap pocket calculators retailed in U.S.

John Fairchild, publisher of *Woman's Wear Daily*, launches new paper, *W*, for "the beautiful people" in U.S.
Corduroy jeans and skin-tight, rainbow-colored ribbed sweaters and turtle-necks
Leather chokers and bracelets, threaded with beads
Headbands: striped sweatbands for sporty types, bandannas and Indian block-prints for hippies

71

First Strategic Arms Limitation Treaty (SALT) agreement is reached at Moscow summit
People's Republic of China enters United Nations
War breaks out between India and Pakistan
Nation of Bangladesh is created
Ten guards and 32 prisoners are killed when police storm Attica prison in N.Y. State following five-day uprising

New films include: *A Clockwork Orange* and *Love Story*
Andrew Lloyd-Webber and Tim Rice musical *Jesus Christ Superstar* opens
Bangladesh Benefit Concert in Central Park, New York, is initiated by ex-Beatle George Harrison
Britain's currency is converted to decimal system
Jim Morrison, lead singer of The Doors, dies

Hot pants galore—in satin, velvet, etc.; sometimes worn with maxi-length coats
Cartridge belts for would-be cowboys and heavy-metal musicians

72

U.S. President Richard Nixon visits Beijing, China
Berlin Wall is opened to allow family visits
Leaders of Baader-Meinhof gang of terrorists are arrested in Germany
Murder of Israeli athletes at Munich Olympics by Black September terrorists

David Bowie releases *Ziggy Stardust* album
Rocky Horror Picture Show hits the stage
Japan develops new synthetic fibers; advancing strength and aerodynamics of industrial clothing
U.S. bans use of the pesticide DDT

Widely flared "loon" pants
1920s and 1940s revival clothes at Biba in London
Handpainted leather bags, silk shirts, appliqué
Pants tucked into knee-length boots
Colorful cropped tank-tops (sleeveless pullovers)

73

Britain, Denmark and Ireland admitted to European Economic Community (EEC)
Vietnam cease-fire; U.S. troops withdrawn; military draft ends in U.S.
Military coup in Chile
Yom Kippur Arab-Israeli war; Arab states raise oil prices and embargo oil to U.S.
Israel and Egypt declare cease-fire; Middle East peace talks open in Geneva

American baseball star Roberto Clemente dies
Senate opens Watergate hearings
Hit singles are released by teen favorites The Osmonds, David Cassidy, Bay City Rollers

Glam shiny suits and make-up for men on stage
Embroidered kaftans, Indian shirts and gauze smocks
Simply cut dresses in new synthetic jersey
Boom in T-shirts printed with political and advertising slogans
American Lauren Hutton becomes highest paid model in history

74

Ethiopian emperor Haile Selassie deposed
India explodes its first atom bomb
Civil war breaks out in Cyprus
British mainland bombings by Irish Republican Army
U.S. President Richard Nixon resigns

Alexander Solzhenitsyn goes into exile in the West
Film *Stardust*, starring Adam Faith and David Essex, about self-destruction of a successful pop group, released
Blazing Saddles, a spoof of western films, opens
North Sea oil begins to flow

"Granny" clothes and collarless "grandfather" shirts
Suede "creepers" shoes with thick soles: part of the rock 'n' roll revival
Designer knitwear: new elegance and richness of pattern; encourages interest in hand-knitting and picture sweaters

75

Communists take over Cambodia and South Vietnam; the last Americans leave as Saigon falls
Mozambique and Angola become independent
British electorate votes in EEC referendum
Emperor Haile Selassie dies
Civil war in Lebanon and Angola

Blockbuster film *Jaws* released
International Women's Year proclaimed; Sex Discrimination Act introduced in Britain
Bruce Springsteen's first hit, *Born to Run*, released
Fashion press includes more articles on alternative technology, promoted by energy crisis

Cheap and radical chic: second-hand baseball jackets: army fatigues in khaki camouflage
Fiorucci fun clothing
Clingy dresses flaring just below the knee
Anti-fur lobbying: fake furs gain popularity
Giorgio Armani sets up on own as design consultant

76

United States observes Bicentennial
Israeli commandos rescue airline passengers hijacked at Entebbe, Uganda, by PFLP guerrillas
Riots in Soweto, South Africa
Mao Ze-dong dies
Unemployment rises in Britain and U.S.

Race Relations Act introduced in Britain
Queen, Elton John and Abba enjoy big commercial successes
Bob Marley's album *Rastafarian Vibration* released
Extremist right-wing National Front confrontation at Notting Hill Carnival, London
Gases from spray cans reported to damage the ozone layer

Exercise clothing: Lycra leotards
Punk Festival at London's 100 Club
Expansion of clothing and textile manufacture in developing countries, and some Free Trade Zones

77

Charter 77, a human rights manifesto, is published in Czechoslovakia
Queen Elizabeth II celebrates Silver Jubilee in Britain
Steve Biko, black trade union leader, dies in police custody in South Africa
Mogadishu, Somalia, hijacking of Lufthansa plane by Baader-Meinhof terrorists; hostages released by West German antiterrorist force
Egyptian president Anwar Sadat visits Israel
London–New York passenger service on Concorde jet begins

Sex Pistols' *God Save the Queen* banned by the BBC
Elvis Presley dies
Roots, American TV mini-series, aired
U.S. skateboarding craze spreads to Europe, hotly pursued by roller discos

Punk anarchy: safety pins, ripped and torn second-hand clothes, plastic, leather
American preppie and Ivy League styles increasingly popular in Japan, as well as in U.S.
Diane Keaton dresses in Ralph Lauren trouser suits in Woody Allen film *Annie Hall*

78

China's Premier Hua announces Four Modernizations
Amoco Cadiz disaster results in massive oil slick in the English Channel
Menachem Begin and Anwar Sadat agree to Camp David Accords for Mideast peace
Democracy Wall in China
Diplomatic relations opened between U.S. and the People's Republic of China
World's first test tube baby born

"Winter of Discontent" grips Britain as strikes for substantial wage settlements are called
Saturday Night Fever, is hit film of the year, reflecting discomania craze
Running marathons turn into big public events

Perry Ellis launches own sportswear label
Women's executive fashion: tailored coats, "unconstructed" jackets and padded shoulders
Punk style glamorized and tamed in new wave fashion

79

Shah of Iran abdicates; Iran becomes Islamic Republic
U.S. embassy in Teheran seized; 63 staff taken hostage
Vietnamese depose Pol Pot regime in Kampuchea (Cambodia)
Margaret Thatcher becomes British prime minister
General Anastasio Somoza of Nicaragua overthrown
Russians invade Afghanistan

Sex Pistol Sid Vicious dies from drug overdose while awaiting trial for alleged murder
Woody Allen's film *Manhattan* premieres

More than 30 brands of designer label jeans are on the market
Design consciousness grows; need to dress well (more conventionally) for work
"New Romantic" fantasy dressing takes hold on weekends, on stage, or after dark
Sony Walkman introduced

Siouxsie Sioux, dressed to kill. Her "Gothic" make-up and hair were developed as a dramatic stage style; they represent new wave glamour, rather than the radical, anarchic punk which they are often – mistakenly – associated with.

Index

Figures in *italics* refer to illustrations.

Albini, Walter *34*
American Graffiti 5
Annie Hall 57
Armani, Giorgio 57, 60
art & artists 20
Ashe, Arthur 17
Ashley, Laura *10*, 32, 60

Balenciaga, Cristobal 32
Barthes, Roland 8
Beene, Geoffrey 52, 60
Benatar, Pat 41
Bendel, Henri 25
Biba 25, *34*, 60
black culture 17, 36
Blahnik, Manolo 49
Blass, Bill 52, 60
Bolan, Marc *42*
Bowie, Davie 40-1, *43*
Broadhead, Caroline *51*
Brown, James 36, *36*
Burrows, Stephen 25
Byrne, David 20

Cardin, Pierre *24*, 56, 60
Chelsea Cobbler 49
The Clash *47*
classics, back to 57
Cohn, Nik 53
Cooper, Alice 44
Cosmopolitan 10
crafts 18, *18*
Crosby, Denise *53*

dancewear 52-4
de Niro, Robert 44
denim 28, *30*; *see also* jeans
Denisoff, R. Serge, *Solid Gold* 23
Dior, Christian *9*
disco dancewear 52-4
Divine 14, 15
djellabah 33, 60
Doobie Brothers *30*

Eco, Umberto, 'Lumbar Thought' 8
environmental concerns 8, *8*, 15, 17
Erker, Richard 41
ethnic look 18, 33-5
exotica *26*

fashion, rules of 24
Fawcett, Farrah *15*
Feraud, Louis 10, *11*
films 5; *see also* under titles
Fiorucci, Elio 49, *50*, 60
Fixx, James F., *The Complete Book of
    Running* 17
Fonda, Jane 55
Fraser, Kennedy 24, 52
Frink, Elizabeth 20
Frizon, Maud 49

Gernreich, Rudi 52
Gibb, Bill *56*, 60
Glitter, Gary 22
The Godfather 32
Graham Central Station *38*
Grease 6, 53
The Great Gatsby 5, 32
Greer, Germaine, *The Female Eunuch* 10

Halston 56, 60
Harry, Debbie 44
Hayes, Isaac *22*
Hechter, Daniel *13*, *50*, 60
Hell, Richard 44, *45*
Hendryx, Nona 41, *43*
hippies *9*, 28, *29*
Hockney, David 20
Howell, Georgina 15
Hughes, Patrick 20
Hynde, Chrissie 41

Irwin, Colin 32

Jackson Five 23
James, Tony 15
Jarman, Derek, *Jubilee 27*
jeans 12, 25, *31*; designers' 49, 56
John, Elton 49, *51*
Jubilee Year 27

Kamali, Norma 41, *43*, 60
Klein, Calvin 56, *58*, 60
Kops, Marion *53*

Lagerfeld, Karl 57, *59*, 60
Lauder, Estée 17
Lauren, Ralph *10*, 32, 57, 60
Lear, Amanda 40
leather 29
LeGaspi, Larry 41, *43*
Lehr, Henry 28
Lennon, John 32
Lovich, Lene 44
Lurie, Alison 12

Marley, Bob *39*
McLaren, Malcolm 27, 44
menswear *24*, 25, *25*
Mercury, Freddie 41
Metropolitan Museum of Modern Art 32
Miyaki, Issey 57, *57*, 60
Mohawk hairstyle 44
Mooshamer, Rudolf *33*
Mori, Hanae 33, 60
Morrison, Jim 28
Mr Freedom 25
Muir, Jean 57, *59*, 60
music 22-3, 28; glam-rock 40-3, *42-3*, *63*

The New York Dolls *47*
Nixon, Richard M. 7, *7*
nostalgia 5, *6*, 24, 32-5

The Osmonds *21*, 22

Page, Jimmy 18
pant suits 12

Plant, Robert 41
Porter, Thea 17, 25, 60
preppie look 8, 32-3
Presley, Elvis 32
Price, Antony 40, 60
Punk 44-7, *45-7*

Reger, Janet *12*
Reich, Charles, *Greening of America* 15
Reid, Jamie 27
Rhodes, Zandra 41
Rocky Horror Picture Show 40
Rolling Stones 28
Ross, Diana *39*
Rotten, Johnny 22, 44, *45*
Roundtree, Richard *16*, 17
Roxy Music 40
Ruffin, Clovis 25
Rykiel, Sonia 25, 60

Saint Laurent, Yves 33, *35*, 49, 60
Santana *37*
Sarah Lou 41
Saturday Night Fever 53, *54*
Schumacher, E.F., *Small is Beautiful* 15
second-hand clothes 15
Sex Pistols 22, 44, *45*
Shaft 16, 17
Sims, Naomi 36
Siouxsie & the Banshees 45, *63*
skinheads 12
Slade 22, 41
The Slits 44
Sloane Rangers 8
Sly, J.B. 22
Smith, Patti 44
Smith, Willi 52, 60
Spare Rib 10
sports/jogging 52-5
Springsteen, Bruce *30*
Stewart, Rod *27*, 41
Styrene, Poly 44, *47*
Summer, Donna *39*

Taxi Driver 44
terrorism 13, *13*
tough guys 29-31
trash culture 48-51, *48*, *49-51*
Travolta, John *6*, 53, *54*
Tree, Penelope *34*
The Tubes 44

Van Peebles, Melvin 17
Vanderbilt, Gloria 56
Village People 29, *31*
Vogue 15, 24, 32
Von Fürstenberg, Diane 57, 60
Vreeland, Diana 32

Warhol, Andy 20, 28
Watergate scandal 7, *7*
Westwood, Vivienne 27, 44
Wolfe, Tom 5, 22, 29, 36
women's movement 10, 12

York, Peter 8
Yuki *19*, 20, 60